Shaking Your Generation

Also by Joseph Achanya

Signs and Wonders Follow You

Shaking Your Generation

Shaking Your Generation

The Believer's Call to Global Impact

Joseph Achanya

Without limiting the rights under copyright(s) reserved below, no part of this publication may be reproduced, stored in, or introduced into a retrieval system or transmitted in any form or by any means (electronic, mechanical, photocopying, recording, or otherwise) without the prior permission of the publisher and the copyright owner.

The content of this book is provided "AS IS." The publisher and the author make no guarantees or warranties as to the accuracy, adequacy, or completeness of or results to be obtained from using the content of this book, including any information that can be accessed through hyperlinks or otherwise, and expressly disclaim any warranty expressed or implied, including but not limited to implied warranties of merchantability or fitness for a particular purpose. This limitation of liability shall apply to any claim or cause whatsoever, whether such claim or cause arises in contract, tort, or otherwise. In short, you, the reader, are responsible for your choices and the results they bring.

The scanning, uploading, and distributing of this book via the internet or any other means without the permission of the publisher and copyright owner is illegal and punishable by law. Please purchase only authorized copies, and do not participate in or encourage piracy of copyrighted materials. Your support of the author's rights is appreciated.

Copyright © 2024 by Joseph Achanya. All rights reserved.

Released November 2024
ISBN: 978-1-64457-724-0

Rise UP Publications
644 Shrewsbury Commons Ave
Ste 249
Shrewsbury PA 17361
United States of America

www.riseUPpublications.com
Phone: 866-846-5123

Unless otherwise noted, all Scriptures are from the KING JAMES VERSION, public domain.

Scripture quotations marked (NLT) are taken from the Holy Bible, New Living Translation, copyright ©1996, 2004, 2015 by Tyndale House Foundation. Used by permission of Tyndale House Publishers, Carol Stream, Illinois 60188. All rights reserved.

Scripture quotations marked (NIV) are taken from THE HOLY BIBLE, NEW INTERNATIONAL VERSION®. Copyright© 1973, 1978, 1984, 2011 by Biblica, Inc.™ Used by permission of Zondervan.

Scripture quotations marked (ESV) are from the ESV® Bible (The Holy Bible, English Standard Version®), copyright © 2001 by Crossway, a publishing ministry of Good News Publishers. Used by permission. All rights reserved.

Scripture quotations marked (NRSV) are taken from the New Revised Standard Version Bible, copyright © 1989 the Division of Christian Education of the National Council of the Churches of Christ in the United States of America. Used by permission. All rights reserved.

Contents

Introduction 9

Part One
Go

Chapter 1 13
I Am God's Choice

Chapter 2 19
I Go With You

Chapter 3 25
The Global Mission

Chapter 4 31
Hear the Cry

Chapter 5 35
Hurry Up

Chapter 6 39
All Expense Paid Trip

Chapter 7 45
Sir, Yes Sir

Part Two
The Message

Chapter 8 49
The Message In Detail

Chapter 9 55
The Center Attraction Of The Message

Chapter 10 61
The Simplicity Of The Message

Chapter 11 65
The Power Of The Message

Chapter 12 71
Boldness

Part Three
Infallible Proof

Chapter 13 77
Where Is Your Approval?

Chapter 14 81
The Full Gospel

| Chapter 15 | 85 |

The Recipe For Taking Territories

| Chapter 16 | 91 |

This Same Jesus

Part Four
Hindrances

| Chapter 17 | 97 |

Severe Criticism And Persecution

| Chapter 18 | 99 |

Choosing To Please Men

| Chapter 19 | 101 |

Talked Out

| Chapter 20 | 103 |

Arrival Mentality

| Chapter 21 | 105 |

Killing The Delivery Man

| Afterword | 107 |

| Signs and Wonders Follow You | 109 |
| About the Author | 113 |

Introduction

As thou hast sent me into the world, even so have I also sent them into the world.

— John 17:18

Jesus, during His 33 years of life, focused solely on ministry for only three and a half years. However, the global impact He made in those three years cannot be denied; He shook the world.

The Apostles, taking over after Jesus, continued with the same intensity, shaking their generation. It was even said that they turned the world upside down (Acts 17:6). Now, it is our turn. In our hands rests the sacred baton passed down through the ages. Jesus expects us to carry forward the mission and maintain the same intensity of impact.

In this book, I unveil the secret recipe that Jesus and the Apostles utilized to shake their world, leaving an enduring legacy that resonates to this day. Why should we seek to substitute an already proven method? The value of this book

Introduction

lies in its ability to reveal the pattern needed to impact and transform your generation, allowing you to fulfill your mission. It serves as a radiant torch, guiding millions of believers, gospel workers, Bible students, preachers, and ministers and enabling them to become global Apostles, Evangelists, Pastors, Prophets, and Teachers. You possess everything necessary to shake your generation. Read this book and leave an indelible impact on your world.

Part One

Go

Chapter One

I Am God's Choice

NOT QUALIFIED FOR THE JOB

Every time God sends a person on a mission, the feeling of unworthiness is often the first thing they have to deal with. Jeremiah, when called by God, expressed his doubt, saying, *"Ah, Lord God, I am only a child and do not know how to speak"* (Jeremiah 1:6). Similarly, Moses, when chosen by God, responded, *"Please, Lord, I have never been eloquent; I am slow of speech and tongue"* (Exodus 4:10). Gideon, too, questioned his worthiness, saying, *"Oh my Lord, how can I save Israel? My family is the weakest in Manasseh, and I am the least in my father's house"* (Judges 6:15). And when Jesus called Peter, he exclaimed, *"Go away from me, Lord, for I am a sinful man!"* (Luke 5:8).

The feeling of unworthiness arises when God selects someone for a mission precisely because He never gives a person a mission that they can handle on their own. The task is always greater than the individual. God told Gideon that he would defeat the Midianites *"as one man"* (Judges 6:16).

Joseph Achanya

Imagine that! Jesus entrusted the spreading of the gospel to just twelve men, expecting them to carry it to the ends of the earth. This is seemingly impossible by any logical standard.

The vision is always greater than the person. How can one person fill the shoes of Jesus in their generation? How can they bridge the gap and show their generation that Jesus is alive and active today, just as He was in Bible days? It may seem like an insurmountable task, a big shoe to wear for someone with small-sized feet.

Imagine if God looks upon the nation of China and declares, "You, as one individual, shall shake this entire nation." Or if God turns His gaze toward Africa and tells you, "Through your efforts, Africa shall be saved," echoing the words spoken to Reinhard Bonnke. Initially, they all exclaimed, "The vision is bigger than us." Yet, it is in those moments of feeling inadequate that God displays His power and ability to achieve the impossible.

THE BEST MAN FOR THE JOB

Guess what? If God has chosen you for a specific task, then you are undoubtedly the best person for the job. You are the vessel that God has selected to shake continents like Africa, Asia, and America. You are God's appointed healer for this generation, entrusted with carrying His miraculous power to nations. No one else can fulfill this role better than you. God has a grand project, a mission of great significance in countries such as America, India, Indonesia, Nigeria, Ghana, and South Africa. And He has specifically chosen to partner with you. In His eyes, you are the best person for this job.

Just like there was no doubt that Oral Roberts was the best man to build a world-class university for God, or Reinhard

Shaking Your Generation

Bonnke was the best man to witness the salvation of over 75 million souls in Africa, or T.L. Osborn was the best man to carry God's miraculous power and impact nations, there is no doubt that you are the best person for the task that God has called you to undertake. Embrace this truth and step into your divine calling with confidence, knowing that God has handpicked you for this purpose.

HE CHOSE YOU

You see, in the powerful words of John 15:16, Jesus tells us, *"Ye have not chosen me, but I have chosen you and ordained you..."* It's important to not only speak about our faith in God, our belief in Him, and our decision to serve Him, but we must also recognize God's unwavering faith in us and His belief in our abilities, even before we make a conscious decision to follow Him. Before we even realized it, God had already chosen us and entrusted us with great tasks because He knows that we won't falter or disappoint. His belief in us is profound.

If we were to have a conversation with God, we might find ourselves asking, "Why would you choose to entrust the task of spreading the gospel to the ends of the earth to just a few, like us?" In response, Jesus would lovingly assure us, "Because I trust you. I believe in you." God's faith in us is astounding, to the point that He has placed all His confidence in us, displaying just how much He truly believes in us. The burning passion within us to shake nations with the transforming power of the gospel did not originate from our own strength—it was God who planted that fire within our hearts. Our deep desire to witness our generation saved and changed is simply a response to God's initial decision to choose us. He personally handpicked us to be His partners in this divine

Joseph Achanya

mission. Let us remember that it was not us who chose Him; rather, He is the one who chose us.

IN HIS EYES

Do you see yourself the way God sees you? If God has such unwavering faith in you, why don't you recognize the incredible potential He sees in you? He sees all the qualities needed to make a profound impact on a generation within you. Can you see that too?

In Jeremiah 1:7, the Lord reminds Jeremiah, *"Do not say, 'I am only a child,' for to everyone I send you, you must speak."* Although Jeremiah saw himself as a mere child, God saw him differently. Similarly, Peter saw himself as a sinful man in Luke 5:8, but Jesus encouraged him not to fear, saying, *"From now on you will catch men."* God perceives you differently as well; He sees you as the perfect candidate for the task at hand.

REDEEMED FOR THE JOB

Refuse to let the devil condemn you any longer.

Devil: You are not qualified to heal the sick; you need healing yourself.
Me: I am the redeemed of the Lord, chosen to carry God's miraculous power.

Devil: You are not qualified to save Africa; you need salvation yourself.
Me: God came down, saved me, and washed me in His blood to equip me for this mission. I am the redeemed of the Lord.

Shaking Your Generation

Devil: You are not qualified to impact this generation; you will be overcome.
Me: I possess all that is necessary to influence my generation; I am the redeemed of the Lord.

Devil: Who do you think you are to come here and achieve what no one else has?
Me: I am the redeemed of the Lord.

Devil: I give up.
Me: That is precisely why I was sent—to put you in your place and exalt Jesus.

GOD'S LAST MEN

We find ourselves in the critical juncture of the end times, with the imminent folding of the earth. As the last representatives entrusted with the baton, God has placed great reliance on us to complete the task at hand. It is our responsibility to bear the saving and healing power of Jesus to the countless souls yet unreached and nations yet untouched. The triumph of the church in this relay race hinges upon the swiftness with which we run. The Apostles, serving as God's pioneers, ran with incredible speed. In just two years, the word of the Lord spread throughout Asia, reaching both Jews and Greeks (Acts 19:10).

This swift progress was witnessed by even the Pharisees, who admitted, *"You have filled Jerusalem with your doctrines"* (Acts 5:28). Such was the velocity of their mission. Now, the baton has been passed on to us, chosen by God as the final emissaries to carry His miraculous power and revolutionize our generation.

Chapter Two

I Go With You

Lo, I am with you always, even unto the end of the world. Amen.

— Matthew 28:20

IN THIS TOGETHER

God did not send you to win your world and shake your generation only to sit back and watch you fail. You are partnered with God in this endeavor. It is His business and assignment that you are carrying out, so you are never alone. God is your partner in the task of shaking the world. He commanded you to go, and He goes with you. God arrives when you arrive, and He takes action when you begin to act. This assurance was given to the apostles, and we have the same assurance today because we share the same assignment. In Mark 16:15-20, it is stated, *"Go ye into all the world, and preach the gospel to every creature. He that believes and is baptized shall be saved, but he that believeth not shall be damned. And these signs shall follow them that believe: In my*

Joseph Achanya

name they shall cast out devils; they shall speak with new tongues. They shall take up serpents; and if they drink any deadly thing, it shall not hurt them; they shall lay hands on the sick, and they shall recover. So then after the Lord had spoken unto them, he was received up into heaven, and sat on the right hand of God. And they went forth, and preached everywhere, the Lord working with and confirming the word with signs following." Every command from God is accompanied by His assurance of His presence going with you and in you. It does not matter where He sends you, He is there with you. Whether it is India or America, a village or a town, Nigeria or Dubai, you can be assured of His presence with you. When you enter a community, God visits that community through you. Imagine what you and God can achieve together as partners in any city. That is why the result in every city you visit should be the same: "The city was shaken." You and God, together, shook that city.

Whenever God has an agenda for a generation, He chooses partners from that generation. God is a spirit and needs flesh to carry out His agenda in that city. The flesh also needs the spirit to carry out God's agenda. The equation is simple: God's spirit plus your flesh equals nations being shaken. You and God are in this together. In 2 Corinthians 6:16, it is written, *"And what agreement hath the temple of God with idols? For ye are the temple of the living God; as God hath said, I will dwell in them, and walk in them; and I will be their God, and they shall be my people."* God dwells in you, walks in you, and is your God. You are His partner. He partnered with the apostles, and they shook their generation. He partnered with T.L. Osborn and shook his generation. He partnered with Oral Roberts, and together, they built a world-class university. He partnered with Paul, and they performed special miracles together. Acts 19:11 states, *"And God wrought special miracles by the hands of*

Shaking Your Generation

Paul." This verse perfectly explains your partnership with God.

God worked the miracles, but the people saw Paul's outstretched hands because God is a spirit and Paul is flesh. Even today, God wants to heal the sick, but He is looking for partners who can stretch out their hands. God wants to shake nations and save generations, but He needs human partners. God wants to partner with you. You and Him together. Many believers have not understood the concept of partnership with God. That is why their prayers often sound like it is them against God or, at other times, like they are trying to get God on their side. "Oh God, please go with me" or "Oh God, don't leave me" may no longer feel right when you discover that God made the first move. Preachers pray and try to convince God to move in their meetings or to heal the sick and save the people, forgetting that the battle is not them against God, but them and God against sickness and every oppression of the devil. Over 2,000 years ago, God made the first move to save His people, to heal them, and to end the oppression of the devil. You are only just entering into His plan now, so stop sounding like you are more interested in the people than God is. You are not alone. You and God are partners in the business of shaking nations.

> *For he hath said, I will never leave thee, nor forsake thee.*
>
> *— Hebrews 13:5*

God will not abandon you in the middle of the assignment He has commissioned you to do. He is there with you in the inner city, in the Arab Nations, and at every point. You are never alone, so never feel like you can't continue or that

Joseph Achanya

the assignment is too big for you to handle alone. God is on your side. Together, you and God make an unbeatable team.

GOD'S NEW ADDRESS

God once resided in a physical form known as Jesus of Nazareth, but now, He resides within you. In the words of John 14:10 (NIV), Jesus proclaimed, *"Do you not believe that I am in the Father and the Father is in me? The words I say to you I do not speak on my own authority. Rather, it is the Father, living in me, who is doing his work."*

Just as Jesus acknowledged that His life's impact was a result of the Father dwelling in Him, now the Father has chosen to dwell in you. It is through you that God continues to carry out His work, just as He did with the body of Jesus. The God within you is the same God who dwelled within Jesus, performing the same miraculous works. Jesus serves as our example, as the first human vessel inhabited by God, showing us what we can aspire to be, what we can accomplish, and how our ministries and lives should reflect the presence of God within us.

You are currently God's dwelling place, His headquarters. He has taken hold of you to reveal Himself to the world through you. Colossians 2:9-10 (NIV) states, *"For in Christ all the fullness of the Deity lives in bodily form, and in Christ you have been brought to fullness. He is the head over every power and authority."* Today, it brings joy to the Father that His fullness and presence dwell within you. The eternal God has made His abode in you, and wherever you go, you carry Christ with you, impacting every community you encounter. Just as Mary carried Jesus within her during her pregnancy, traveling from place to place, we too carry Jesus within us.

Shaking Your Generation

God through Christ in Bible days, Christ through you today. As stated in 1 John 4:4 (NIV), *"You, dear children, are from God and have overcome them because the one who is in you is greater than the one who is in the world."* No nation can overpower you, for you carry within you the Creator of the universe, the God of the heavens and the earth.

GOD-INSIDE MINDED

If you want to make a lasting impact on your generation, it is essential to maintain a consciousness that God lives within you. This consciousness is crucial for living a life that exceeds mediocrity.

There are two ways to cultivate this awareness:

1. See Christ in you always, through faith

Scripture tells us that Christ dwells in our hearts through faith (Ephesians 3:17). Faith allows us to perceive what our physical eyes cannot see. When I step onto a platform to minister, I may not physically feel the presence of God within me, but I have learned to see Him through the eyes of faith. My faith is built on His promise never to leave or forsake me. Despite not feeling any physical sensation, I have laid my hands on the sick and witnessed blind eyes opening, deaf ears hearing, and the lame walking. This is because I see God working through me by faith. When you consistently see Christ dwelling within you, nothing will be impossible for you. Relying solely on feelings will not provide a consistent flow of miracles in your life, as feelings can be unreliable.

2. Declare Christ in you

As Jesus moved through His earthly ministry, He made known His union with the Father. John 14:10 states, *"Do you*

Joseph Achanya

not believe that I am in the Father, and the Father is in me? The words that I speak to you I do not speak on my own. But the Father who dwells in me does His works." In John 10:30, Jesus affirms, *"I and the Father are one."* Likewise, in John 17:21, He expresses, *"...as You, Father are in Me, and I in You."* As generation shakers, we have the privilege of speaking in the same manner Jesus did, for we are now God's dwelling place. Continually declare, "God lives in me! I am an overcomer!" I have made this proclamation countless times, embracing the truth that God resides within me always.

REDEEMED TO CARRY GOD

God purged us from our sins so that He could dwell within us. The sole reason we have the privilege of carrying God is because our sins have been forgiven. God specifically chose you, washed you in His blood, and transformed you into a new person. Only as a new creation do you possess the capacity to carry God within you. Place your trust in the fact that Jesus paid the ultimate price for your sins, and as a result, you have a right, acquired through His precious blood, to carry God within you.

Chapter Three

The Global Mission

For the Son of Man came to seek and to save the lost

— Luke 19:10 (NIV)

SEEKING AND SAVING

Being sent on a global mission is about wearing the shoes of Jesus and continuing the ministry that He began.

Jesus' entire life revolved around people. He came for people, lived for people, and ultimately died for people. This mission is centered around souls, as there is a battle on earth between light and darkness for the salvation of mankind. Everything else in this world will pass away, but the souls of people are eternal. To make an eternal impact, you must go after that which is eternal. God has chosen you to join His army. If you are not winning the lost, it is essential to reassess your purpose because God has not called anyone to a ministry that does not involve winning souls. This global

Joseph Achanya

mission is all about rescuing people from darkness and bringing them into the light.

I am personally invested in depopulating hell and populating heaven. I am constantly strategizing on how to fulfill the Great Commission to *"Go."* What actions are you taking to win the lost? If every individual is actively pursuing lost souls, an entire nation can be transformed. The quickest way to lose your ministry and sense of purpose is to stop reaching out to the lost. This is the primary reason why God sends you to any nation. When you arrive, direct your focus toward seeking and saving the lost. Cultivate a passion for those who are in spiritual darkness. Although charitable acts are biblical and valuable, they cannot change nations. What is the point of clothing a body that will eventually perish anyway? If you desire to have a lasting impact, you must prioritize souls.

If soul-winning is not currently a priority, make a conscious effort to change that. Follow the example of T.L. Osborn and implement strategies such as literature evangelism, which is utilizing written materials to spread the gospel message far and wide. He impacted his generation through his soul tracks translated into different languages. Consider television evangelism, using media platforms to communicate the gospel, just as Billy Graham became known worldwide through his televised specials. Another powerful method is one-on-one evangelism, which involves face-to-face encounters and sharing the gospel with individuals directly. This approach is exemplified in biblical accounts such as Philip and the Ethiopian eunuch (Acts 8) and Paul speaking to King Agrippa (Acts 26).

Crusade evangelism, also known as mass evangelism, is a style of reaching the lost by inviting people en masse to public gatherings. In these settings, a message of salvation is

Shaking Your Generation

preached, and individuals are given the opportunity to accept Jesus as their Lord. Some may argue that this form of evangelism is impersonal and ineffective, but I can assure you that it works. I have witnessed transformed lives and heard countless testimonies of people finding hope and a new life in Christ through such crusades. What is your preferred approach? Are you actively making an effort to reach the lost? Choose from these strategies or employ them all. This is the essence of the mission at hand.

WINNING THE WORLD

The mission is global because the instruction is to *"...go into the (entire) world and preach the gospel to every creature"* (Mark 16:15).

God has sent you with a message to the world. A true evangelist wants to win the world for Jesus. If the instruction for the mission says every creature, it means if there is still one soul yet to be saved, the mission is incomplete.

Every individual deserves a fair chance to hear the gospel and be allowed to accept or reject Christ. This is why the vision is for every kindred, every people, every tongue, every nation, every tribe (Revelation 7:9).

> *Ye shall receive power, after that the Holy Ghost has come upon you, and ye shall be a witness unto me in Jerusalem, Judaea, Samaria, and unto the uttermost part of the earth.*
>
> *— Acts 1:8*

The vision is one person at a time, one city at a time, one nation at a time until the whole world hears the message. It is okay to start small, but the vision must be global. Develop a burning passion for world evangelism—this is the mindset of nation-shakers. There are billions of people who have never heard the gospel, which means there is still work to be done.

> *And this gospel of the kingdom shall be preached in all the world for a witness unto all nations; and then shall the end come.*
>
> *— Matthew 24:14*

Every single soul matters to God. The Bible says, *"God is not willing that any should perish"* (2 Peter 3-9). So God has a mission for all the world. How about you? How far do you want to go? How many cities do you want to cover? Whenever you think of the gospel, you must see all nations.

MOBILE MISSION

Jesus Christ was an itinerant preacher, constantly on the move. He traveled throughout cities and villages, preaching in synagogues and spreading the gospel of the Kingdom. Alongside His preaching, He also performed miraculous healings, bringing relief to those suffering from various sicknesses and diseases (Matthew 9:35).

Jesus understood that His impact could not be limited to one city or confined to a specific village. His mission was to reach everyone, everywhere. This awareness is evident among influential individuals who have left a lasting impression on their generations. They were all mobile preachers, individuals who recognized the necessity of spreading their impact worldwide. For example, T.L. Osborn preached in more than

Shaking Your Generation

78 nations, Benson Idahosa traveled to 145 countries during his lifetime, and Billy Graham shared the message of the gospel in over 185 nations.

Sitting in the comfort of a church office will not enable you to shake a nation. It is imperative to start moving! Once you have impacted one nation, do not become complacent. Seek guidance from God to identify the next city that needs your influence.

Keep moving until your voice is heard and your presence is felt in every nation across the globe. The mission is global, and thus, one must be mobile.

Understand that there will be no respite until every individual has heard the gospel. As long as you have breath in your lungs, you must continue to move. Remain committed to the global mission and be willing to travel far and wide, reaching every corner of the world with the message of salvation. Mobility is key to fulfilling the calling and making a significant difference.

Chapter Four

Hear the Cry

IF YOU ARE OUT THERE

We often speak of Christ's second coming. Yet, there are millions who have never even heard of His first coming. Why should someone hear the gospel twice when others haven't heard it once? Dr. Morris Cerullo once shared a poignant story from his travels. Along the way, he stopped in a village to quench his thirst and purchased a drink from a man selling Coca-Cola. Curiously, he asked the man if he had heard about Jesus. The man responded, "No, is it another brand of Coca-Cola?" This encounter reminded Dr. Cerullo of the incredible ignorance that exists, where Coca-Cola has spread, but the message of Jesus has not reached. The realization brought him to tears, reflecting on the reality that revolutionary products and ideas have reached places where the church has failed to make an impact. It is a cry that resounds from nations, and if we truly hear it, we cannot help but join in that cry ourselves.

Joseph Achanya

Here is another story I recently heard: A preacher, simply exploring the features of his Google map, stumbled upon a place where people lived, far beyond the reach of other humans. Intrigued, he felt compelled to find a way to reach them. Although the process took him two painstaking years, his determination paid off, and he finally arrived.

As the people saw him, the entire village emerged, eager to know his purpose. When asked, he replied, "I have come to tell you about the God who sent His Son to die." Astonishingly, the villagers immediately dropped to their knees and began to weep. The king stood up and told him that two years ago, they thought in their hearts that life must be beyond them and there must be a God out there so they came out every night, faced the sky, and cried, "If there is a God out there, send somebody." He wasn't aware of their prayers, but God sent him in answer to their prayers. This story serves as a powerful reminder that God sends us to nations in response to their cries. Someone, somewhere, is desperately calling upon God to reveal himself, and God can answer that plea through us. We are the answers to the prayers of countless families and nations throughout the world.

LISTEN AND YOU WILL HEAR

> *And a vision appeared to Paul in the night: a man of Macedonia was standing there, urging him and saying, 'Come over to Macedonia and help us.' And when Paul had seen the vision, immediately we sought to go on into Macedonia, concluding that God had called us to preach the gospel to them.*

> *— Acts 16:9-10 (ESV)*

Shaking Your Generation

Paul listened and heard the cry of the Macedonian people calling for help. You too can hear the cry of nations if you listen. Nations are crying for help, and you have the answer. Open your spirit, and listen. Sick people are crying for help; open your spirit and listen. Do not ignore the cry of families, the cry of cities and nations calling you to come to their rescue. Ask God to show you where to take the next crusade, and then listen. You will hear where the need is most urgent. You are God's answer to the cry of many.

> *And when the Lord saw that he turned aside to see,*
>   *God called unto him out of the midst of the bush*
>   *and said, Moses, Moses. And he said, here am I,*
>   *And He said, Draw nigh hither: put off thy shoes*
>   *from off thy feet, for the place whereon thou*
>   *standest is holy ground. Moreover, he said, I am the*
>   *God of Abraham, the God of Isaac, and the God of*
>   *Jacob. And Moses hid his face; for he was afraid to*
>   *look upon God. And the Lord said, I have surely*
>   *seen the affliction of my people which are in Egypt,*
>   *and have heard their cry by reason of their*
>   *taskmaster; for I know their sorrow, And I am*
>   *come down to deliver them out of the hand of the*
>   *Egyptians and to bring them up out of that land*
>   *unto a good land...*

— *Exodus 3:4-8*

You see that the call of Moses was in response to the cry of the Israelites to God. Even so, the call of God on your life is in response to the cry of the nations to Him. God is calling you to respond on His behalf. Demonstrate on his behalf, go on His behalf!

Joseph Achanya

LOOK AND YOU WILL SEE

The truth is, you don't need a special call, vision, dream, or revelation to recognize the need for the gospel in your surroundings. Simply open your eyes, and you will know where to go and whom to reach out to. Many people have asked me how I determine where to hold the next crusade, questioning if I rely on an audible voice, dreams, or revelations. Most often, my answer is this: I open my eyes, observe where the need is greatest, and take action.

The great commission requires us to go into all the world, so we keep going until we sense a divine restraint, just as Paul experienced in Acts 16:6.

T.L. Osborn once said, "Lord, if there is a specific field, area, or nation where You want to guide us, show us, and we will go. But if You do not, we will choose the best opportunity to reap the greatest harvest, where there are the fewest laborers, and we will be there reaping until You direct us elsewhere."

Do not turn a blind eye to the need for the gospel around you. Do not act as if you cannot see the sinner living right next to you or the sick person in your midst. Why are you waiting for an audible voice or a revelation before laying hands on the sick? Open your eyes, discern the need, and act on God's behalf. The call of God will always amplify the needs in your vicinity. Others may pass by the person in a wheelchair without seeing the problem, but not you. There might be believers in the same nation who are indifferent to the gospel in a specific region, but not you. Look, and you will see; listen, and you will hear the cries of the nation.

Chapter Five

Hurry Up

*And another angel came out of the temple, crying with
a loud voice to him that sat on the cloud, Thrust in
thy sickle, and reap: for the time is come for thee to
reap; for the harvest of the earth is ripe.*

— Revelation 14:15

THE HARVEST IS READY

Allow the urgency of this mission to resonate within
you. You cannot afford to be found doing anything
other than the work to which God has called you. Excuses
are not an option. The harvest is ripe, and the people are
eagerly waiting. The sick and oppressed have waited for far
too long. Time is running out, and you must act with haste.

Remember, the account God wants to hear is that of the
mission He sent you to carry out on earth. The One who sent
you is coming back soon. I hope you will have delivered His
message when He returns.

35

Joseph Achanya

THE LAST HOUR

Dear children, the last hour is here. You have heard that the Antichrist is coming, and already many such antichrists have appeared. From this, we know that the last hour has come.

— *1 John 2:18 (NLT)*

We find ourselves on the brink of the return of the One who sent us. We are closer to the culmination of all prophecies than ever before. The fulfillment of these prophecies serves as a catalyst for His imminent return. As mentioned in Matthew 24:7, nations will engage in conflict with one another, and famines and earthquakes will afflict various parts of the world. These signs further highlight the proximity of the end times; however, many remain unaware of just how close we are to this significant period.

With limited time at hand, we find ourselves faced with an abundance of tasks. The harvest is ripe, yet the number of laborers is insufficient. Consequently, we must hasten our efforts and intensify our commitment. It is crucial to be fully engaged during this final hour. Our focus must be fixed solely on delivering the message we have been entrusted with, without allowing anything to divert our attention.

In John 9:4, Jesus reminds us that we must diligently work on the tasks assigned to us by the One who sent us while there is still daylight. A time will come when preaching and spreading the Word will no longer be possible—a time referred to as the night hour—a period when the message loses its relevance. The approach of this night hour is swift, and therefore, we must act with urgency. Let us be spurred

Shaking Your Generation

into action by the awareness that time is rapidly dwindling. The night is approaching, the doors will soon close, and the opportunity to make a lasting impact will be gone. May this realization motivate us to redouble our efforts and strive to fulfill our mission with zeal and effectiveness.

YOUR END

Some might disbelieve this world may end, or if there's even an end, we are close to it. Let's assume these assumptions are true. There is another important fact that is being ignored. That is, even if someone does not believe that we are close to the night hour, it is a fact that we are closer to our life's end. As a human being, death is an assurance you have. Even if the world never ends, your life will end. You don't have the luxury of time. Reinhard Bonkke said, "The gospel is eternal, but you don't have eternity to preach it." The harvest is ready, and the night hour is near, so we must hurry up.

Chapter Six

All Expense Paid Trip

WHO PAYS THE BILL?

It is a common concern for those who are called by God to participate in global missions to worry about finances. It is understandable that they often worry about finances and seek support from various sources, such as financial aid or writing appeal letters for funds, because the task at hand is often greater than what our bank accounts can handle. However, it is important to remember that God does not consider our financial capabilities before assigning us a mission. He looks at His own ability to provide.

God does not want us to be preoccupied with the burden of financing His mission. He never called us to rely solely on our own resources. I once experienced this realization during a meeting as part of an organization's executive team. The president gave one of us the task of delivering letters to numerous companies in the city. The person immediately expressed concern, stating that they did not have the finances

Joseph Achanya

to cover all the expenses. The president responded reassuringly, saying, "Whenever I assign you a task, do not worry about finances. The organization will take care of the expenses." Those words struck a chord within me. Whenever God sends us on a mission, we need not worry about lacking money.

I also learned a meaningful analogy that reiterates this point. It involves a four-year-old child who answered the door to find a representative from the electricity company handing them the monthly bill. The child became worried upon seeing the amount to be paid and was unable to sleep at night due to anxiety. The mother, awakened by her distressed child, inquired about the problem. The child responded, "The electricity company brought the bill, and I have been worried." The mother then explained, "Why didn't you give me the bill? It is not your responsibility to pay but mine." Many times, this analogy has reminded me that I do not have to shoulder the financial burdens of the mission; it is God's responsibility.

GWADA GOOD NEWS CRUSADE

This was the second crusade I organized in the city of Gwada, located in the northern part of Nigeria. As we were preparing for the event, I requested every department to provide me with a comprehensive list of all the necessary items and expenses. However, as our ministry was still in its infancy, there was no money in our bank account, and we didn't even have a bank account established yet. After compiling all the bills, it became evident that we couldn't afford to proceed with the crusade. However, we had already announced our arrival, and the city was eagerly anticipating our coming.

Shaking Your Generation

With only a few days left until the crusade, everyone kept questioning how we were going to proceed and if the event would still take place as planned.

Two nights before the crusade, I sat outside my house listening to a sermon titled "Performance of the Word." I became worried, but at that very moment, God spoke to my heart. He said, "I will send you to Gwada for free." The next morning, an amazing surprise awaited me. I received a message on my phone that said: "I just got your account number from a friend, and I just transferred money to your account." To my astonishment, the exact amount needed for the crusade had been deposited! That is what an all-expense paid trip means. God pays His bill!

GOD PAYS HIS BILLS

When God gives an order, He also provides the means to fulfill it. Every mission trip is fully funded by God. Just like when God sent the seventy disciples (Luke 10:1-4), He appointed them and sent them out two by two into every city and place where He Himself intended to go. He reminded them that the harvest was plentiful but the laborers were few, so they were to pray to the Lord of the harvest to send more laborers. He instructed them to go on their way, but without carrying a purse, bag, or sandals, and not to greet anyone on the road. This was a clear indication that they were not to rely on their own provisions or resources. God specifically told them not to bring anything with them, emphasizing that if He was the one sending them, He would take care of the expenses.

To demonstrate His commitment to paying His bills, He asked them upon their return, "When I sent you without purse, bag, or sandals, did you lack anything?" And they replied, "Nothing" (Luke 22:35 NIV). They went empty-handed but didn't experience any lack because God is faithful to His promise of providing.

Nehemiah didn't finance the building of the wall (Nehemiah 2:2-9).

Moses didn't finance the construction of the tabernacle (Exodus 25:1-8, Exodus 36:5-7).

Ezra didn't finance the building of the temple (Ezra 1:1-4).

The pattern remains the same. God pays for what He orders. He has assured you of sending you around the world, so there is no need to fear, because just like always, God is committed to paying His bills.

You can liken yourself to a builder. Builders don't fund their own projects. The one who gives the order to build also provides the materials and pays for the labor. In the same way, when God gives you an assignment, He will provide everything you need to fulfill it. Trust in His faithfulness to cover all the expenses.

GOD IS NOT CONCERNED ABOUT THE COST OF ANYTHING

The bill is not yours to pay, so why worry? Do you doubt that God can finance the vision He has given you? Are you concerned that the budget exceeds God's capabilities? If that is your worry, then let it go. God is not concerned about the cost of anything.

According to the riches of His glory, He can afford far more than your budget allows. God knows the vision and its

Shaking Your Generation

requirements before placing it in your heart. Why would He call you to do something He cannot provide for? Every time you worry, you underestimate God's ability to finance what He orders. Rest assured, all the provisions you need to fulfill your vision are well within God's capabilities.

Chapter Seven

Sir, Yes Sir

COMMISSION NOT SUGGESTION

In Mark 16:15, Jesus instructs His disciples to go into all the world and preach the gospel to every creature. It is important to note that the Great Commission is not mere advice, but a command, as emphasized by Reinhard Bonkke. Therefore, we must treat it as such and respond with obedience.

Kenneth Copeland, in his desire to follow God's commands, humbly declares, "I am yours to command." Similarly, Paul shares his encounter with King Agrippa, recounting how the Lord appeared to him on his journey to Damascus and gave him specific instructions. Paul's response to God's command was one of complete obedience, as he stated, *"Whereupon, O King Agrippa, I was not disobedient to the heavenly vision"* (Acts 26:19).

Just as Paul responded with unwavering obedience, so should we approach the Great Commission. It is a call to action that

Joseph Achanya

demands our immediate attention. Let us imagine a dialogue between God and ourselves:

God: Go into the world!
You: Sir, yes sir.

God: Preach the gospel to every creature.
You: Sir, yes sir.

God: He that believes and is baptized shall be saved, and he that does not believe shall be condemned.
You: Sir, yes sir.

God: In My name, cast out devils.
You: Sir, yes sir.

God: In My name, lay hands on the sick, and they shall recover.
You: Sir, yes sir.

God: In My name, you shall be protected from harm.
You: Sir, yes sir.

This should always be our response to the Great Commission (Mark 16:15-18). May we embrace this call with humility and determination, fulfilling our role as disciples of Christ by spreading His message and demonstrating His power through our actions.

Part Two

The Message

Chapter Eight

The Message In Detail

THE FAULTY GOSPEL

If we preach a faulty gospel, our convention will also be flawed. It is crucial that we accurately communicate the gospel. You must understand that it is not your message to craft; there already exists a message. All you have to do is preach it. There are two kinds of extremes regarding evangelism. Some have the correct message but fail to preach it, while others are eager to preach but lack the right message. Be careful not to fall on either side of the ditch. A faulty gospel is a powerless gospel, and it cannot produce the expected result. If you don't preach what the apostles preached, you won't see what the apostles saw in the Book of Acts.

WHAT IS THE GOSPEL?

*Moreover, brethren, I declare unto you the gospel which
I preached unto you, which also ye have received,*

Joseph Achanya

> *and wherein ye stand; By which also ye are saved,*
> *if ye keep in memory what I preached unto you,*
> *unless ye have believed in vain. For I delivered unto*
> *you first of all that which I also received, how that*
> *Christ died for our sins according to the scriptures;*
> *And that he was buried, and that he rose again the*
> *third day according to the scriptures:*

> *— 1 Corinthians 15:1-4*

This is the gospel that shocked the world, the gospel that Paul received and Peter preached, the gospel that prevails. The first notable detail we see in this gospel is that Christ died for our sins. If you don't preach the cross, there is no gospel. Billy Graham once shared a story of how he preached at a crusade but felt no power or impact. Only a few people came forward to make a decision for Jesus. When he came down from the platform, he was concerned about his lack of power, so he asked his crusade director what had gone wrong. The crusade director responded, "You didn't talk about the cross." It was on the cross that Jesus took us, and whoever believes in Him shall not perish. The death of Jesus is good news for all people because all have sinned, as the Bible declares in Romans 3:23. The wages of sin is death, which is why everyone deserves to hear the gospel. When a person hears the gospel, they rejoice because they discover that their sins have been paid for and they no longer have to die in their sins.

> *For the wages of sin is death; but the gift of God is*
> *eternal life through Jesus Christ our Lord.*

> *— Romans 6:23*

Shaking Your Generation

It was on the cross that His blood was shed for us. It was on the cross that He died our death and paid the wages of our sins. The only way Jesus could pay for our sins was to die. He died a vicarious death on the cross for all of humankind. His death was the atoning price for the sins of the world, and

> *This is a faithful saying, and worthy of all acceptation,*
> *that Christ Jesus came into the world to save*
> *sinners; of whom I am chief.*

> — *1 Timothy 1:15*

> *Since the wages of man's sin have been paid for, man*
> *has been reconciled with God.*
> *For if, when we were enemies, we were reconciled to*
> *God by the death of his Son, much more, being*
> *reconciled, we shall be saved by his life.*

> — *Romans 5:10*

The gospel is Good News to all men. As the Bible declares in Romans 3:23 (NIV), "For all have sinned and fall short of the glory of God." The wages of sin is death, which is why everybody deserves to hear the gospel. When a man hears the gospel, he rejoices because he discovers that his sins have been paid for. He no longer needs to run away from God but can now freely turn to Him. This is the good news that brings man back into a restored relationship with God.

> *And all things are of God, who hath reconciled us to*
> *himself by Jesus Christ, and hath given to us the*
> *ministry of reconciliation; To wit, that God was in*
> *Christ, reconciling the world unto himself, not*

Joseph Achanya

> *imputing their trespasses unto them; and hath
> committed unto us the word of reconciliation.*

> — *2 Corinthians 5:18-19*

If you exclude the payment for our sins through the death of Jesus, you are preaching a different gospel. Another powerful detail in this message is the resurrection. In Acts 8:5, we see Philip going to Samaria and preaching about Christ. The central theme of our message is Christ, and if it fails to reveal Him, then it has been altered. Christ is the only message we should be proclaiming in the world today.

> *And daily in the temple, and in every house, they
> ceased not to teach and preach Jesus Christ.*

> — *Acts 5:42*

The primary message entrusted to the early church by Jesus Christ is Jesus Christ Himself. This is the only message that has been passed down to us by the early church, and it should not be altered, added to, or taken away from in order to maintain its power and effectiveness. When we preach Jesus Christ, we will experience results. This was the message preached by the early church, and it produced great works.

I have personally preached this message, and I have witnessed its power working effectively every day and in every place. The resurrection on the third day is the pinnacle of the gospel's power. Our Savior not only died but also rose from the dead after three days, providing tangible proof of His teachings. Death has claimed the founders of every other religion, but Jesus was buried in

Shaking Your Generation

Israel, as the Bible states. If you visit Mecca, you will find the grave of Mohammed, but if you go to Israel, where Jesus was buried, His tomb is empty, confirming the truth of His resurrection.

> *And as they were afraid, and bowed down their faces to the earth, they said unto them, Why seek ye the living among the dead? He is not here, but is risen: remember how he spoke unto you when he was yet in Galilee.*
>
> — *Luke 24:5-6*

Our redeemer lives! The eternal significance of our redemption should never be overlooked when it comes to the gospel. The resurrection of Christ is vital and undeniable proof that our gospel is true and trustworthy. If Jesus did not rise from the dead, our gospel would lack credibility and legitimacy. Therefore, we must always uphold the truth of Christ's resurrection as an essential part of the gospel message.

> *And if Christ be not raised, your faith is vain; ye are yet in your sins.*
>
> — *1 Corinthians 15:17*

Christianity distinguishes itself from every other dead religion precisely because of the resurrection. Without the resurrection, Jesus Christ would be just like any other ordinary figure from history. However, the resurrection is what sets Jesus apart. It is what makes Him the same yesterday, today, and forever, as Hebrews 13:8 declares. The resurrection is not a mere historical event; it is breaking news that brings life-altering transformation.

Joseph Achanya

A man who died and rose up after three days, never to die again. This extraordinary detail cannot be overlooked or excluded from the gospel. It is the heart of the message, offering everlasting life to all who believe in Him. Every detail in the gospel is crucial and interconnected. Removing even one aspect affects its entire framework. Jesus died for our sins, just as the Scriptures foretold. He was buried, and on the third day, He rose again, all in fulfillment of the Scriptures. This is the message that God confirms with signs, wonders, and miracles, for it is the message He has sent us to proclaim to the world.

Chapter Nine

The Center Attraction Of The Message

And the things that thou hast heard of me among
many witnesses, the same commit thou to faithful
men, who shall be able to teach others also.

— *2 Timothy 2:2*

FAITHFUL MESSENGER

God has sent us to the world on a global mission, where each messenger has a unique and vital message to deliver. Our role is not that of an entertainer or comedian; rather, we are individuals who carry a message of salvation, healing, and deliverance. As faithful messengers, it is our duty to diligently fulfill this responsibility.

Joseph Achanya

WHAT QUALIFIES ME TO BE A FAITHFUL MESSENGER?

Ensure that the message is received on time

A while ago, I was planning for a program and sent invitation letters via the post office to friends of the ministry. Unfortunately, most of the letters were not delivered until after the event, so when the information got to them, it was of no use anymore. The message we are given has a time frame in which it must be delivered; otherwise, the information is of no benefit to the receiver. This is why we must carry a sense of urgency in delivering the message that was committed to our hands. Another time, I wanted to use a church to hold a miracle meeting. I sent a letter to the church requesting to use their church facility, and to date, the letter hasn't been delivered, and the meeting has never been held. This is the case for some messengers. They get distracted and involved in doing many things other than delivering the message. Giving yourself to distractions disqualifies you from being a faithful messenger. Distractions delay you, and sometimes, they will stop you.

Ensure that the message is delivered accurately

It is not up to us to create our own message. We are not to speak anything else other than what the Lord commands. This is one of the reasons letters are sent with seals so that the content of the letter is not altered. God told Ezekiel:

> *And he said unto me, Son of man, go, get thee unto the house of Israel, and speak with my words unto them.*
>
> — *Ezekiel 3:4*

Shaking Your Generation

A faithful messenger is only supposed to speak God's message and not his own.

- Don't worry about how the message sounds, preach it!
- Don't try to make the message more appealing, just preach it!

We must resist the temptation to modify or share other messages, as Paul emphasized to the Galatian church. (Galatians 1:6) By staying true to the message we are given, we can expect God's power to be manifested. The only message that God confirms is the gospel.

Expect to live the message that you deliver

Our actions speak louder than words, and our credibility as messengers is closely tied to our conduct. If we are hypocritical or rebellious, people may not listen to or follow the message we deliver. It is essential to understand that others are watching us, and our behavior can either attract or repel them from the message. We must be cautious not to cause anyone to stumble or hinder them from embracing the message. Hypocrisy has no place in being a messenger of God, as we are called to authentically live out the message we proclaim.

THE HIM BOOK

The whole Bible is a "Him" (Christ) book.

Search the scriptures; for in them ye think ye have eternal life: and they are they which testify of me.

— *John 5:39*

Joseph Achanya

The testimony of Christ is seen from Genesis to Revelation. If you read the Bible and you don't see Christ, you need to put on your "Son" glasses. Christ is the central message of the Bible. Someone may be thinking, "But Jesus wasn't born until Matthew." Yes, you are correct! Jesus was physically manifested in Matthew, but He has always been in the Scripture through types and shadows. Jesus confirmed this while preaching a message after His resurrection to the two men on their way to Emmaus.

> *Then he said unto them, O fools, and slow of heart to believe all that the prophets have spoken: Ought not Christ to have suffered these things, and to enter into his glory? And beginning at Moses and all the prophets, he expounded unto them in all the scriptures the things concerning himself.*

> *— Luke 24:25-27*

Jesus affirmed that the Old Testament writings, from Moses (Genesis to Deuteronomy) to the prophets (Major and Minor Prophets), bear witness to his suffering (death) and subsequent glorification (resurrection). In fact, the story of Jesus unfolds throughout the pages of the Old Testament. Thus, by delving into the Old Testament, one can discover a comprehensive account of Jesus' life, fulfilling the prophecies and promises of God.

- The Messiah will perform miracles. (Isaiah 35:5)
- He will ride on a donkey into Jerusalem. (Zachariah 9:9)
- He will be betrayed by his friend. (Psalm 41:9)
- The betraying friend will be paid 30 pieces of silver. (Zachariah 11:12-13)

Shaking Your Generation

- He will be beaten, mocked, and spat on. (Isaiah 50:6)
- Lot will be cast for his clothing. (Psalm 22:18)
- He will not defend himself. (Isaiah 53:7)
- He will be crucified. (Psalm 22:16)
- He will be crucified with sinners. (Isaiah 53:12)
- None of His bones will be broken. (Psalm 34:20)
- He will be forsaken by God. (Psalm 22:1)
- He will die. (Isaiah 53:8)
- He will resurrect. (Psalm 16:10)
- He will ascend into heaven. (Psalm 68:18)
- He will sit at the right hand of God. (Psalm 110:1)

In the Old Testament, Christ was concealed in types and shadows, and Christ was revealed in substance in the New Testament. Great ministries are judged by their extent of knowledge about Christ.

- OLD TESTAMENT – Prophecies of His coming
- GOSPELS – Manifestations of prophecies
- EPISTLES – Announcement about Him
- REVELATION – He is coming back again
- HE PREACHED CHRIST

Then Philip opened his mouth, and began at the same scripture, and preached unto him Jesus.

— *Acts 8:35*

When I die, I want it inscribed on my gravestone that "He preached Christ"

— *Reinhard Bonnke*

Joseph Achanya

Christ is not just at the center of our message; He is our message. During the early days of the church, the Apostles proclaimed Christ incessantly, and this remains true today. Christ is the focal point of our preaching, and His presence resonates with everyone who listens. His teachings, life, death, and resurrection form the core of our faith. Christ is not simply a part of our message; He is the very essence of it.

> *And daily in the temple, and in every house, they*
> *ceased not to teach and preach Jesus Christ.*

> — *Acts 5:42*

The message entrusted to us is solely centered around Christ. When we preach Christ, it has the power to impact and resonate with people everywhere, regardless of location or circumstances. We have one gospel to share, and its essence remains consistent across boundaries. So, there is no need to be concerned about delivering elaborate or fancy sermons; the focus should always be on preaching Jesus Christ. As the apostle Paul declared, he resolved to know nothing among the people except Jesus Christ and his crucifixion.

> *For I determined not to know any thing among you,*
> *save Jesus Christ, and him crucified.*

> — *1 Corinthians 2:2*

Paul preached Christ. If we preach what the apostles preached, we shall experience what the apostles experienced. I want it to be said that I too preached Christ.

Chapter Ten

The Simplicity Of The Message

THE FOOLISHNESS OF PREACHING

In His infinite wisdom, God has chosen a method of revelation that goes beyond human understanding. He has decided that the world would not come to know Him through human wisdom alone. Instead, He has used what may seem like foolish preaching to save those who believe, as mentioned in 1 Corinthians 1:21.

When the gospel is preached in its original form, it may sound foolish to the audience. This is why King Festus accused Paul of being insane and claimed that his learning was driving him to madness, as stated in Acts 26:24. The message Paul was delivering seemed foolish to Festus.

How could the death of one man possibly save the world? How could a man rise from the grave after being buried for three days? Yet, this seemingly foolish message is the wisdom of God at work. Instead of allowing the entire human race to perish, God chose to manifest Himself in the flesh,

61

Joseph Achanya

die on our behalf, and offer salvation to whoever believes in Him.

Many have attempted to make the gospel sound more appealing and reasonable, but as Paul described it, it is the "foolishness of preaching." It may sound foolish, but it is powerful. It may sound foolish, but it produces power. If we try to simplify the gospel, it will remain profound. The result will still be simple yet impactful.

MAJOR ON WHAT MAJORS

Sometimes, we only have about four minutes to deliver a message, so it's important to focus on the main points and avoid unnecessary details. This might be the person's only chance to hear the gospel, so we don't want to waste it by trying to sound reasonable. This is the core message of the gospel:

- God's creation (Perfection)
- Satan's deception (The fall of man)
- Christ's substitution (The cross)
- Our restoration (Reconciliation)

Understanding these concepts is all that is needed to preach the gospel to the nations. This is what truly works and what God confirms.

SPIRITUAL MATURITY

Spiritual maturity does not mean that nobody can understand you. Spiritual maturity does not involve isolating oneself in doctrinal ecstasy. As T.L. Osborn stated, we should not aim to preach in a manner only theologians can comprehend. The

Shaking Your Generation

power of the gospel lies in its simplicity. Preaching should not be about impressing others. It is a grave mistake to alter the message in order to impress people or yourself. If everyone deserves to hear the gospel, it should be presented in a way that everyone can understand. True spiritual growth is demonstrated when one finds the simplest way to communicate the gospel with people from all walks of life. Do not let your spiritual maturity hinder the spreading of the gospel quickly.

> *But I fear, lest by any means, as the serpent beguiled*
> *Eve through his subtilty, so your minds should be*
> *corrupted from the simplicity that is in Christ.*

> *— 2 Corinthians 11:3*

Do not fall into the trap of the devil, which seeks to remove the simplicity of the gospel from you in the name of spiritual maturity. There may be a temptation to believe that there must be more to the message. Thoughts may arise that the message is incomplete and should be explored further. However, whenever you add or remove elements from the gospel, you are challenging the wisdom of God.

The gospel is founded on the idea that we must accept its foolishness and preach it in its original, unchanged form. Do not be swayed by the devil's deception and instead hold fast to the simplicity and purity of the gospel message.

Chapter Eleven

The Power Of The Message

*...for, "Everyone who calls on the name of the Lord
will be saved." How, then, can they call on the one
they have not believed in? And how can they
believe in the one of whom they have not heard?
And how can they hear without someone preaching
to them? And how can anyone preach unless they
are sent? As it is written: "How beautiful are the
feet of those who bring good news!" But not all the
Israelites accepted the good news. For Isaiah says,
"Lord, who has believed our message?" Consequently, faith comes from hearing the message, and
the message is heard through the word about
Christ.*

— Romans 10:13-17 (NIV)

Joseph Achanya

THE POWER OF THE MESSAGE

We bear the weight of the most crucial message on Earth today. Salvation comes by hearing the gospel because one cannot call upon the Lord without first believing. And belief cannot be achieved without first hearing the message. It is important to understand that salvation does not come from people's prayers alone, but it is through the preaching of the gospel that individuals find their redemption. We must realize that someone else's salvation is in our mouths.

ETERNAL DESTINY

Whenever the gospel is preached, it becomes a pivotal moment of decision. It is the moment you decide your eternal destiny. It is the moment you decide if you will spend eternity in heaven or hell. There are so many ways to hell, but there is only one way to heaven. This is the exclusivity of the gospel. In the gospel is the power to save you from hell and death. Someone's eternal destiny is determined by whether you are a faithful messenger or not, how fast you get the message to them, or if the message gets to them at all. Delivering the message on time is the perfect help you can give to any man. The gospel is eternal, but we don't have eternity to preach it.

Timely delivery of the message is the greatest assistance we can offer to anyone. The gospel itself is timeless, but we have limited time to preach it. People may not express gratitude because they have yet to understand the importance of prioritizing their eternal needs over their immediate desires. When we knock on their door, carrying the message we were sent to deliver, they eagerly open it, anticipating a package that could

Shaking Your Generation

fulfill their immediate needs, such as food, money, or clothing. However, once we begin to share the message of the gospel with them, their enthusiasm diminishes. They fail to realize that this is a matter of life and death, a matter of where they will spend eternity. This message has the power to save them from the torment of hell; it contains the very essence of God's salvation. The greatest support we can provide to others is not limited to material provisions like food, clothing, or money. After all, what good is it to feed a body that will inevitably perish? What purpose does it serve to clothe an individual who will forever remain naked in eternity?

While you may quench their thirst with water in this earthly life, in eternity, they will forever yearn for a single drop of water. We are the bridge between hell and heaven, for how can someone believe in someone they have never heard of?

And how can they hear about Him without a preacher?

THE SOLUTION TO THE WORLD

I pray that mankind would come to realize how lost they are without God. They live with undiagnosed ailments, problems without solutions, diseases without remedies, guilt without forgiveness, and a lack of peace. However, the gospel holds the answer to all of these struggles. We possess what the world truly needs; we hold the key to their questions and uncertainties. While the world remains in darkness, the gospel brings forth light. As mentioned in Ephesians 5:8, we were once in darkness but now walk as children of the light in the Lord. The god of this world has blinded the minds of those who do not believe, preventing them from seeing the light of the glorious gospel of Christ, who is the image of God (2 Corinthians 4:4). The world is trapped in bondage,

Joseph Achanya

but the gospel offers freedom. Colossians 1:13 states that God has delivered us from the power of darkness and has brought us into the Kingdom of His dear Son.

The world is lost and has misplaced priorities, but the gospel has the power to find them and give them purpose. The apostle Paul wrote in 2 Corinthians 4:3, *"But if our gospel be hid, it is hid to them that are lost."* We have been entrusted with the most powerful message in the world, one that can bring light to the darkness, freedom from bondage, and direction to the lost.

WHOSOEVER

The power of the gospel lies in its ability to be received by whosoever believes.

> *...that whoever believes in him shall not perish but have eternal life.*
>
> *— John 3:16 (NIV)*

> *For the scripture saith, Whosoever believeth on him shall not be ashamed.*
>
> *— Romans 10:11*

> *For whosoever shall call upon the name of the Lord shall be saved.*
>
> *— Romans 10:13*

Shaking Your Generation

*For whosoever shall do the will of God, the same is my
brother, and my sister, and mother.*

— *Mark 3:35*

*But whosoever drinketh of the water that I shall give
him shall never thirst.*

— *John 4:14*

*Whosoever shall confess that Jesus is the Son of God,
God dwelleth in him, and he in God.*

— *1 John 4:15*

Anyone can be whosoever! Anyone who believes the gospel shall be saved! There is no discrimination in the gospel. It does not exclude anyone based on their status. No one is too lowly to be saved by the gospel, and no one is too esteemed to be outside of its reach. In Acts 10:34 (ESV), when Peter realized that even the Gentiles were included in the "whosoever," he declared, *"Truly I understand that God shows no partiality."* Therefore, we must never withhold the gospel from anyone for any reason. They are all part of the "whosoever" and deserve the opportunity to hear the message that can bring salvation.

Chapter Twelve

Boldness

Lo, I am with you always, even unto the end of the world. Amen.

— Matthew 28:20

UNASHAMED

The power of the gospel is undeniable, and I believe it should be shared unashamedly. I have witnessed first-hand the mockery and ridicule that often follow the preaching of the gospel. People scoff at the existence of God and laugh at the idea of believing in something they cannot see. They mock the exclusivity of the gospel, questioning how anyone could claim that there is only one way to God. Even the resurrection, a cornerstone of our faith, is met with ridicule and disbelief. But just because they lack under-standing doesn't make the gospel any less true. I firmly believe that one day, those who mock will come to know the truth that we have been preaching. I refuse to be ashamed of the gospel of Christ (Romans 1:16). Jesus himself faced

Joseph Achanya

mockery, as did the apostles Peter and Paul. They were called insane and faced increasing opposition in their time. But they were not deterred. Their boldness only intensified as they proclaimed the truth fearlessly. Intimidation is a common obstacle when preaching the gospel. People often try to intimidate us, threatening or trying to scare us into silence. It can be disheartening, but overcoming intimidation requires boldness. Faced with threats, I choose to stand firm and continue to preach. I don't let discouragement or the words of others stop me from sharing the gospel. Instead, I seek God's strength and pray, just as the apostles did in Acts 4:29-30, for boldness to speak His word. The one who sent us is present with us, empowering us with boldness. Fear has no place in our mission. Remember that you are not alone when confronted with opposition and intimidation.

Your purpose surpasses the fear and ridicule. Choose to embrace and intensify your boldness, pressing on even in the face of adversity. I believe that the gospel is for everyone, and it is our responsibility to share it with boldness and conviction. Do not let the mockery and intimidation deter you from spreading the message of hope and salvation. Because, at the end of the day, it is the truth that sets people free.

CONVICTION

Having conviction is essential for boldness. The apostles were prime examples of men with unwavering convictions, even to the point of being willing to die for what they believed. It is incredibly challenging to resist individuals like them. They cannot be confined to a box, tied down, or demotivated. Furthermore, the true testament of our belief in the gospel lies in the level of intensity with which we hold onto it. The more we believe in the gospel, the more fervently we

Shaking Your Generation

hold onto its principles and teachings. Our conviction becomes evident through our unwavering faith and dedication. In conclusion, boldness stems from deep-rooted conviction, exemplified by the apostles and their unyielding faith. These individuals cannot be constrained or deterred, and our own belief in the gospel is demonstrated through our fervor and determination.

Part Three

Infallible Proof

Chapter Thirteen

Where Is Your Approval?

WHO SENT YOU?

It is not enough to simply say that God has sent you. Anyone can make grand statements, but talk is cheap. When proof is required, people become cautious in their claims. Just like anyone can say that the president sent them, they would face consequences without evidence. Not everyone will believe you solely based on your stating that you were sent by God.

However, when you provide proof of your divine mission, people will believe. In John 14:11, Jesus Himself demonstrated that He was sent by God. Without proof, we are in trouble, but with proof, the devil is the one in trouble.

If people are to believe that you were sent by God, they must not only hear your message but also witness God's approval of that message. Just like Christ's message was accompanied by unmistakable evidence, our ministry today should mirror the ministry of Jesus Christ. A verbal message alone, without

Joseph Achanya

confirmation, is insufficient in bringing about a decision. Therefore, be prepared to present proof that you are indeed.

THE SIGNATURE OF GOD

> *Ye men of Israel, hear these words; Jesus of Nazareth, a man approved of God among you by miracles and wonders and signs, which God did by him in the midst of you, as ye yourselves also know:*
>
> — *Acts 2:22*

Jesus had the approval of God upon His ministry, and the confirmation of God's message was evident in the signs, wonders, and miracles He performed. Signs and wonders are tangible evidence that we are sent by God and that our gospel originated from God.

Even before His resurrection, when Jesus sent out His disciples, He instructed them to provide evidence. This was God's strategy to ensure the smooth spread of the gospel, and it cannot be substituted with any other strategy today.

> *These twelve Jesus sent forth, and commanded them, saying, Go not into the way of the Gentiles, and into any city of the Samaritans enter ye not: But go rather to the lost sheep of the house of Israel. And as ye go, preach, saying, The kingdom of heaven is at hand. Heal the sick, cleanse the lepers, raise the dead, cast out devils: freely ye have received, freely give.*
>
> — *Matthew 10:5-8*

Shaking Your Generation

This is God's strategy: as you go forth and preach, it is not enough to simply deliver the message I have given you. There is more to it. The next step is to demonstrate proof that I have indeed sent you. Miracles, signs, and wonders serve as God's undeniable signature upon a person and their ministry. God desires to reveal to the world that He has commissioned you, and these supernatural manifestations are His chosen strategy for doing so.

THE POWER OF THE MESSAGE

And they went forth, and preached every where, the Lord working with them, and confirming the word with signs following. Amen.

— Mark 16:20

God desires to confirm His message through the power of miracles. One miracle holds the weight and impact of a thousand words. This is exemplified in the story of Moses, where God used signs and wonders to make it clear to Pharaoh that Moses was sent by Him. If signs, wonders, and miracles do not accompany your message, you will encounter difficulties. The reason why there may be ongoing debates about your calling from God is because people have not witnessed the unmistakable evidence of God's signature—the signs, wonders, and miracles—in your life.

Chapter Fourteen

The Full Gospel

*Through mighty signs and wonders, by the power of
the Spirit of God; so that from Jerusalem, and
round about unto Illyricum, I have fully preached
the gospel of Christ.*

— Romans 15:19

PARTIAL GOSPEL

You must continually ask yourself, "Am I a full gospel preacher or a partial gospel preacher?" If you are not a full gospel preacher, then why not? Who is a full gospel preacher? It is someone who proclaims the message of the gospel with signs, wonders, and miracles by the power of the Holy Spirit. If your preaching is not accompanied by miracles, then you have not fully preached the gospel. Refuse to deliver a partial, superficial gospel filled with persuasive words of human wisdom. The demonstration of the Spirit and power is essential. The world has an abundance of eloquent speakers but lacks true messengers who have indisputable

Joseph Achanya

evidence of the gospel. A partial gospel can only achieve so much. It diminishes Christianity, reducing it to a religion without any proof. Muslims do not attend the mosque expecting miracles; instead, they listen to empty repetitions of vain words. They enter blind and leave blind, deaf and leave deaf. They do not anticipate a manifestation of God's power to occur within the mosque. This is precisely what Christianity becomes without a full gospel preacher. The world is seeking individuals who can demonstrate what they preach, not just motivational speakers but true demonstrators of God's power.

PREACHING AND HEALING

The mission of those who are sent has always been to proclaim and demonstrate the message of preaching and healing.

SENT BEFORE RESURRECTION

> *Then he called his twelve disciples together, and gave them power and authority over all devils, and to cure diseases. And he sent them to preach the kingdom of God, and to heal the sick. And he said unto them, Take nothing for your journey, neither staves, nor scrip, neither bread, neither money; neither have two coats apiece.*
>
> *— Luke 9:1-3*

He sent them to preach and heal everywhere—in schools, homes, hospitals, and churches. Anywhere the gospel is proclaimed, it must be accompanied by signs, wonders, and

Shaking Your Generation

miracles. The proclamation of the gospel goes hand in hand with the demonstration of power. Preaching and healing are interconnected; they both proclaim and demonstrate the message of the gospel.

SENT AFTER RESURRECTION

And he said unto them, Go ye into all the world, and preach the gospel to every creature. And these signs shall follow them that believe; In my name shall they cast out devils; they shall speak with new tongues; They shall take up serpents; and if they drink any deadly thing, it shall not hurt them; they shall lay hands on the sick, and they shall recover.

— Mark 16:15, 17-18

The mission remains unchanged—to preach the word and demonstrate its power to the world. This was not a mere coincidence, but rather what set Jesus apart from the scribes and Pharisees. Despite their preaching, Jesus would both proclaim and demonstrate the power of his words.

The former treatise have I made, O Theophilus, of all that Jesus began both to do and teach,

— Acts 1:1

Jesus was not just an ordinary teacher; He captivated people's attention. They saw someone who believed so strongly in what He taught that He demonstrated it in action. If you truly believe in the gospel, you will not hesitate to prove it everywhere you go.

Joseph Achanya

The mission is to both proclaim and demonstrate; one cannot be complete without the other. Any attempt to perform signs, wonders, and miracles without preaching the gospel is merely an ambition to be entertaining. Likewise, preaching without the demonstration of power will ultimately be fruitless. No matter how eloquent your preaching may sound, it is incomplete without the demonstration of power.

The church must not only have conferences centered around the Word but also miracle services. We must go beyond being just learners of Jesus' words; we must also do the works that Jesus did (Luke 5:15). Multitudes followed Jesus for two reasons: to hear the word of God and to be healed. The combination of healing and preaching was central to Jesus' ministry.

> *And Jesus went about all Galilee, teaching in their synagogues, and preaching the gospel of the kingdom, and healing all manner of sickness and all manner of disease among the people.*
>
> *— Matthew 4:23*

This is what a full gospel ministry looks like! You can have a ministry like Jesus did. God wants you to experience what Jesus experienced.

Chapter Fifteen

The Recipe For Taking Territories

BOOK OF ACTS STRATEGIES

The only standard for a biblical ministry is the Book of Acts—nothing less. The believers in Acts were known for their effective strategy of taking the message of the gospel to cities, towns, and villages. This strategy is still relevant today. The apostles' actions in Acts 17:6 were so powerful that, *"These that have turned the world upside down are come hither also;"* They also filled Jerusalem with their doctrine, as seen in Acts 5:28. Paul employed this same strategy, reaching the entire region of Asia within just two years, as described in Acts 19:10. Philip, too, utilized this strategy and captivated the entire city of Samaria, resulting in great joy, as seen in Acts 8:6-8. With such undeniable evidence of success, why should we replace these proven strategies with less effective ones in our ministry today?

Joseph Achanya

> *And with great power gave the apostles witness of the resurrection of the Lord Jesus: and great grace was upon them all.*
>
> *— Acts 4:33*

Their strategy was to witness with great power. Full Gospel was their strategy—proclamation and demonstration were how they did it. Their preaching was accompanied by notable miracles that left no doubt that Jesus was the Christ and had risen from the dead.

For the spread of the gospel in today's world, it is crucial to have preachers who combine their message with powerful demonstrations of signs and miracles. This strategy, known as the full gospel, has the potential to produce the same results as it did in the Bible days. In this generation, there is a great need for miracles, as many people still suffer from incurable ailments. Relying solely on verbal communication to deliver the gospel is not enough to capture the attention of an entire territory. By incorporating both proclamation and demonstration, one can easily attract crowds and effectively deliver the message. When miracles begin to happen, word quickly spreads about what Jesus is doing in these meetings. I have personally witnessed the crowd at our crusades multiply each night as stories of notable miracles spread throughout the city. This strategy remains relevant even in today's generation.

> *All of Jerusalem was attracted to Peter's preaching when the crippled beggar was healed.*
>
> *— Acts 3:9*

Shaking Your Generation

All of Samaria was attracted to Philip's preaching
when they saw the miracles he did.

— Acts 8:5-8

All of Asia heard the Word of the Lord Jesus when they
saw the special miracles God wrought by the hands
of Paul.

— Acts 19:11

All of Ibadan, Nigeria, gave heed to our message when
Karimu, the noted crippled beggar who had
crawled on the ground for thirty years, was
instantly healed.

— T.L. Osborn

And my speech and my preaching was not with
enticing words of man's wisdom, but in demonstra-
tion of the Spirit and of power: That your faith
should not stand in the wisdom of men, but in the
power of God.

— 1 Corinthians 2:4-5

AMPLIFY YOUR VOICE

"When Jesus returned in the power of the Spirit to Galilee, His fame spread throughout the region" (Luke 4:14). As a preacher, if you possess power, your voice will be amplified and your name will become notable, just as Jesus' fame extended to every place in the surrounding country when people witnessed His powerful preaching, the casting out of demons, and the

Joseph Achanya

healing of the sick. If you have a message but nobody is listening because your volume is low, increase the impact of your message with signs, wonders, and miracles. Always leave people with a story to tell at the end of every meeting (Luke 4:37).

> "There was a preacher who resided in a town with a population of merely 120 people. His church had only 10 members. However, when a child died in this small community and he prayed for the child, miraculously raising them back to life, his membership grew from 10 to 100 in a town of 120. The miracle amplified his voice and drew attention to his ministry. Similarly, an evangelist moved to the Philippines with the goal of building a church but had no members. One day, he heard on national news that there was a possessed girl in distress, afflicted by demons. He sought permission to pray for the girl and cast out the demon from her on national TV. As a result, the following week, he gained widespread media coverage. This notable miracle led him to establish the largest church in the world at that time. One remarkable miracle can give voice to your message in every town."

FALSE WITNESS

Any witness without proof is considered false. People will not believe our preaching unless we provide evidence. This is why Jesus recommended that His disciples receive the power of the Holy Ghost before testifying or preaching.

Shaking Your Generation

> *But you shall receive power after the Holy Ghost has*
> *come upon you, and you shall be witnesses to Me in*
> *Jerusalem, and in all Judea and Samaria, and to*
> *the end of the earth.*
>
> — *Acts 1:8*

If you cannot prove the claims of Christ and Christianity, you are a false witness. The claim that Jesus is the Son of God, who died and rose on the third day, requires proof. Nothing can prove His resurrection like power. If Jesus is alive today, He should still be able to perform the same miracles as before—opening blind eyes, raising the dead, casting out demons, and healing lepers. A dead man cannot do these things. Every miracle done in His name is a testament to His resurrection.

> *And with great power, the apostles gave witness to the*
> *resurrection of the Lord Jesus. And great grace was*
> *upon them all.*
>
> — *Acts 4:33*

In this generation, we need proof of the gospel more than the apostles did in their time. What people need now is understanding and evidence, since skepticism has grown. Even by critics, the testimonies of the apostles could be considered credible because they were eyewitnesses to Jesus' miracles, death, burial, and resurrection.

> *That which was from the beginning, which we have*
> *heard, which we have seen with our eyes, which we*
> *have looked upon, and our hands have handled,*

Joseph Achanya

> *concerning the Word of life— that which we have*
> *seen and heard we declare to you.*
>
> *— 1 John 1:1-3*

The apostles were physical witnesses, seeing Jesus ascend into heaven after His resurrection. There is a possibility of accepting their testimony with proof, but for us, who were not eyewitnesses and didn't hear directly from Jesus like they did, we are only believers in the message. This is why Jesus said, *"These signs will follow those who believe"* (Mark 16:17). Any belief without signs following it is a false witness. Why should people accept your message without proof? You were only told a story, not witnessed it yourself. Signs must accompany the preaching of the gospel.

- Heal the sick!
- Raise the dead!
- Clean the leper!
- Cast out devils!

Preach with proof, and it will be easier to share the gospel with the people you were sent to.

Chapter Sixteen

This Same Jesus

Jesus Christ the same yesterday, and to day, and for ever.

— Hebrews 13:8

Throughout my life, I have preached more on this subject than any other. Jesus Christ remains unchanged. His works are the same today. His power is the same today. His ministry is the same today. Jesus Christ is still ministering the gospel.

People who are born today need to see Jesus the same way as people who lived during His time on earth saw Him. He was known as a miracle worker. He was always either on his way to healing the sick, coming back from healing the sick, or healing the sick. It has always been my desire to be known for what Jesus was known for: signs, wonders, and miracles. I want my generation to know that blind eyes still open, deaf ears can still hear, and the dead can be raised back to life again. The apostles' ministry also proved that Jesus is the

Joseph Achanya

same in their generation. There was no difference between Jesus' crusades and Peter's crusades. Multitudes of sick people were brought to Jesus (Luke 4:40; Matthew 4:24), and He healed them all. Multitudes of sick people were also brought to Peter, and he healed them all (Acts 19:12). In fact, Philip's crusade in Samaria was as if Jesus visited Samaria Himself (Acts 8:5-10).

MY ASSURANCE

Every time I step onto the stage, I begin my preaching with a loud proclamation: "Tonight, let the blind expect to see, let the lame expect to walk, let the dumb expect to speak, and let the deaf expect to hear." Why do I promise miracles? Why am I so confident that miracles will happen? Often, there is even a rally around the city before the crusade, announcing that people should bring the sick to the event. What fuels my confidence?

The answer is simple. I believe that Jesus visits every community I do, and He is the same yesterday, today, and forever (Hebrews 13:8). The same Jesus who opened the eyes of the blind, enabled the lame to walk, cleansed the leper, raised the dead, and made the mute speak, is the Jesus I preach. He is alive in me today. If He did it then, He can do it again tomorrow. This is what underpins my confidence; this is why I tell people to expect miracles at my crusade because I preach a God of miracles.

People can change, promises can change, the economy can change, and traditions can change, but the Jesus we preach can never change. You can trust Him.

Shaking Your Generation

THE SAME IN HIS NAME

Everything that the person of Jesus accomplished, the Name of Jesus can achieve. If the person of Jesus is the same today, then so is His Name—the Name of Jesus is equivalent to the person of Jesus. This Name was given to us as proof of His resurrection, and Jesus did not leave us with a name that lacks power. The apostles trusted in it and saw its power; the disciples used it effectively. I have called upon it and witnessed its power, and you too can use it, assured that it will work.

You can use the Name of Jesus to heal the sick, raise the dead, and take nations, just as He did. Jesus left His followers with a name powerful enough to conquer nations, and they did just that. They took the Name of Jesus from town to town, city to city, and village to village, asserting dominion in His name. By doing so, we can demonstrate that He is unchanged today, and our generation shall be profoundly impacted.

Part Four

Hindrances

Chapter Seventeen

Severe Criticism And Persecution

Operating in the supernatural often attracts severe criticism and persecution. Every full gospel preacher has had to confront this challenge. It seems inherent in human nature to attack what is not understood. Many preachers have retreated from the supernatural realm, overwhelmed by criticism. They were labeled as false, beset by lies, and mocked until they could no longer bear it. You might think that healing the sick, casting out demons, or raising the dead would earn you admiration and applause, but often, the reality is quite the opposite. This pattern of rejection has persisted since the time of Jesus, who said, *"Many good works have I shown you from my Father; for which of those works do you stone me?"* (John 10:32). If you aspire to a full gospel ministry, brace yourself for severe criticism. *"If the world hates you, know that it hated me before it hated you"* (John 15:18).

In 2019, a preacher who was reported to have raised the dead on TV faced almost unanimous scrutiny and mockery across TV stations and media blogs. The full gospel's magnetic pull

97

Joseph Achanya

toward severe criticism has deterred many from pursuing it. People who don't know you may spread falsehoods, those intimidated by your ministry might attack you, and individuals who have failed in their attempts might label you a failure.

SEVERE CRITICISM AND PERSECUTION

There are rumors about me that I haven't even encountered myself. Once, at the airport with an old classmate, a photo she shared of us on social media quickly attracted a message cautioning her about associating with me, labeling me as fake. Discovering this was disheartening; I had naively believed I was universally liked, unaware of the narratives painting me as deceitful. On another occasion, when I announced the launch of a radio broadcast named "Full Gospel on Air," I faced an attack from a pastor who claimed I was too young for such an endeavor. He disparaged my plans, suggesting that I should instead give away the planned spending to struggling pastors in villages. Sometimes, criticism stems from jealousy, and other times, from ignorance.

Chapter Eighteen

Choosing To Please Men

Many prefer to stay on the safe side, seeking approval and applause from others rather than facing the harsh criticism that comes with daring steps in ministry. This mindset prevents one from venturing into the supernatural. However, Peter and John posed a crucial question, *"Do you think God wants us to obey you rather than Him?"* (Acts 4:19 NLT), highlighting the importance of divine obedience over human approval. The path to making a difference often involves moving against the current and challenging the status quo. Choosing to please God should always take precedence over seeking favor from people. I've encountered individuals who shy away from supernatural aspects of faith merely to appease skeptics. Yet, God has called me to prophesy, heal the sick, raise the dead, and cast out devils. Regardless of who disapproves, my commitment remains unwavering. The only one with the authority to halt my mission is the One who commissioned me.

Mainstream media opinions, accusations of falsehood, rejection, or criticism do not deter me. What truly matters is not

Joseph Achanya

who stands against me but that God stands with me. His approval is the only validation I seek, and I find assurance in His word.

Chapter Nineteen

Talked Out

Many small ministries we see today began with grand visions, only to have others talk them out of their ambitions. They entered the ministry with dreams of impacting the world and shaking their generation but were persuaded otherwise. This underscores the importance of being selective about whom you share your vision with. For instance, Peter once tried to dissuade Jesus from His sacrifice on the cross.

Frequently, when we arrive in cities for crusades, local skeptics give us numerous reasons why the event won't succeed, citing the failures of past events as evidence. They attempt to measure our potential success by the failures of others. However, we remain undeterred by their skepticism, and by the third night, we often witness the entire city congregating on the field, achieving what was deemed impossible.

In the early stages of every significant project I've undertaken in ministry, there were those who tried to discourage me. They warned me about the high cost of making an impact, claiming it was impossible or too expensive. Yet, I resolved

Joseph Achanya

that if I were to fail, I would fail while attempting something great. Do not let anyone convince you that something is impossible. Indeed, without God, it might be, but we are not without God. With Him, all things are possible! Seeking people's approval for a vision given by God is futile.

Had I waited for human endorsement, I might never have embarked on my ministry journey. The only approval needed to pursue your divine calling is that of God Himself.

Chapter Twenty

Arrival Mentality

There is always more work to be done in fulfilling the Great Commission, which mandates that every creature should hear the gospel. Thus, until your influence reaches every creature and spans the entire world, your mission is far from complete.

The mentality of having "arrived" poses a significant obstacle to expanding one's impact. The accolades and applause that accompany achievements can become a distraction, preventing further efforts. You may be celebrated for winning 1,000 souls, yet you may possess the capacity to reach a million. However, if you let early praise cloud your judgment, you risk stagnating. It's crucial to maintain a relentless desire for more—more souls saved, more sick individuals healed, and more nations touched by the gospel.

As you progress, continually raise the bar. If your initial goal was to reach a million souls and you've reached 700,000, then set your sights on three million. If you've impacted seven nations, aim for fifteen. The objective is never to settle

103

Joseph Achanya

but to keep expanding your goals for the gospel's sake. This relentless pursuit of growth ensures your perpetual relevance in ministry.

Chapter Twenty-One

Killing The Delivery Man

The renowned Scottish pastor Robert Murray M'Cheyne was one of the most impactful ministers in history. Yet, his life was cut short at the age of twenty-nine due to overwork, excessive busyness, and chronic fatigue. On his deathbed, he lamented, "The Lord gave me a horse to ride and a message to deliver. Alas, I have killed the horse and now cannot deliver the message."

This poignant reflection serves as a stark reminder of the importance of self-care in ministry. We are entrusted with a message to deliver, and our bodies are the vehicle for this delivery. Amidst discussions on the necessity of subduing our flesh to nurture our spirit, many preachers are neglecting their physical health to their detriment, risking premature death. It's crucial to care for our physical well-being, as it is the means by which God's message is conveyed.

The Apostle Paul advised the elders of Ephesus, *"Therefore, take heed to yourselves and to all the flock"* (Acts 20:28), highlighting the importance of self-care in effective ministry. However, many fail to heed this advice, embarking on fasts

105

Joseph Achanya

from which their bodies do not recover, thereby underscoring the need for balance. It's imperative to work diligently, but not at the cost of our health. Maintaining a well-ordered life that includes time for rest, days off, vacations, and exercise is not only biblical but also essential. We must attend to our physical health to ensure we can fulfill our assignments to the end.

Afterword

When Peter saw Jesus walking on water, he yearned for his own experience, understanding that one cannot walk on water from within the boat. Unlike the other Apostles who remained seated, he knew he had to step out.

The recipe I have shared in this book won't make any difference until you seek your own experience. You have to go out and prove it. Go and find out if it works! Go and find out what you are made of! Ministry unfolds in two phases: initially, you reach out to the people, and eventually, the world seeks you out. However, this journey begins with the crucial step of *going*.

This generation will continue to tell stories of the previous generations until we step out to seek our own experience. Never be afraid to prove the truth. It always works! The difference between those whose lives will be transformed by this book and those whose will not lies in the willingness to step out, seek firsthand experiences, and put the book's teachings to the test.

Afterword

God desires for you to encounter what Jesus did during His ministry, aiming for you to have a significant global influence. He has laid out a blueprint for you to follow, but the depth of your impact is yours to determine.

Signs and Wonders Follow You
Living a Life of Miracles Daily

And these signs shall follow them that believe...

— Mark 16:17

These were some of Jesus' last words, a promise to anyone who believes in Him: signs and wonders shall follow you. They will follow you to every meeting, every service, and every city, whether you are on the platform or not, whether you are asleep or awake, whether you feel anointed or not.

In Acts 3, Peter prayed for the man who was lame from birth at the Beautiful Gate, commanding him to rise up and walk. This miracle astonished the rulers.

Saying, What shall we do to these men? for that indeed a notable miracle hath been done by them is manifest to all them that dwell in Jerusalem; and we cannot deny it.

— Acts 4:16

Signs and Wonders Follow You

To them, that was a notable miracle. It marveled the entire synagogue. But to Peter, miracles were a daily occurrence. He was surprised that they were surprised.

> *Peter saw his opportunity and addressed the crowd.*
> *"People of Israel," he said, "what is so surprising*
> *about this? And why stare at us as though we had*
> *made this man walk by our own power or*
> *godliness?"*

> — Acts 3:12 (NLT)

We shouldn't be surprised when a miracle happens; we should be surprised when a miracle doesn't happen. Think of it this way: imagine a judge visiting a prison and seeing a criminal he has sentenced. Amazed, the judge asks, "Why are you here?" The criminal replies, "You sentenced me to 10 years in prison." Then, the judge says, "Wow! I didn't think they would put you in prison. I was not feeling well when I made the sentence." It doesn't matter how the judge feels; once he hits the gavel, his words become a decree, and he shouldn't be shocked at the outcome!

Jesus' earthly ministry was full of signs and wonders. Every chapter in the Gospels contains a sign and a wonder. So did the early church. In fact, every chapter in the Book of Acts had a supernatural experience. That's our model: signs and wonders daily. When the Lord called me into the ministry, He said, "Your ministry must be nothing short of the supernatural!" That is God's expectation for every believer.

In this book, I communicate everything I know concerning signs, wonders, and miracles. You will discover how to live a life experiencing miracles everywhere you go. This book will

110

Signs and Wonders Follow You

be a tool in the hands of believers, Bible school students, preachers, and gospel workers to help them exalt Jesus daily.

* * *

Available in Paperback and eBook from Your Favorite Bookstore or Online Retailer

About the Author

Evangelist Joseph Achanya is the founder of Mega Harvest and the host of the "Heal the Sick" radio and TV broadcast. Evangelist Achanya passionately makes Jesus known to today's generation. He has led many international open-air crusades and outreaches under the theme "THIS SAME JESUS," demonstrating the power of the resurrected Christ through signs, wonders, and miracles. Inspired by the ministry of Dr. T.L. Osborn, Evangelist Achanya dedicates his ministry to winning the lost and showcasing the transformative power of Christ. He is a sought-after preacher whose renowned miracle ministry is changing thousands of lives worldwide.

MegaHarvest.org

- facebook.com/preacherjay
- x.com/preacher_jay
- instagram.com/preacher_jay
- youtube.com/PreacherJay

Printed in the USA
CPSIA information can be obtained
at www.ICGtesting.com
LVHW012138161124
796712LV00014B/588